What Color Is Nature?

Stephen R. Swinburne

Boyds Mills Press

Foreword

What color is the sea? What color is the sky? What color is a leaf, a bird, a fish in your hand, and a shell on the beach?

The color of the sea is blue, but sometimes it can look green or black or red or all tipped in white. The color of the sky is blue, but like the sea, it can look white, gray, black, or red. A leaf is green and brown and orange and purple. Birds, fishes, and shells are the colors of beach balls, lollipop, bubble gum, watermelons, and kaleidoscopes.

After a rainstorm, look for a rainbow. Rainbows are made when raindrops reflect sunlight. Can you see these colors in the rainbow: red, orange, yellow, green, blue, indigo, and violet?

What color is nature? Nature is every color you can think of.

—Steve Swinburne

Color is everywhere in nature.

You can see nature's color in many places, such as a baseball field,

at school,

in your backyard,

and in the woods.

Gardens are the very best places to see lots of colors.

There's color on flowers and vegetables.

There's color on moths

and turtles.

There's color in the trees.

Some things are one color.

Some things are two colors.

Some things are many colors.

When you see something, do you know its color?
What color is the grass?

Green.

What's the color of this salamander?

Orange.

What color is this apple?

Red.

What color are these shells?

Black.

What color is this flower?

Purple.

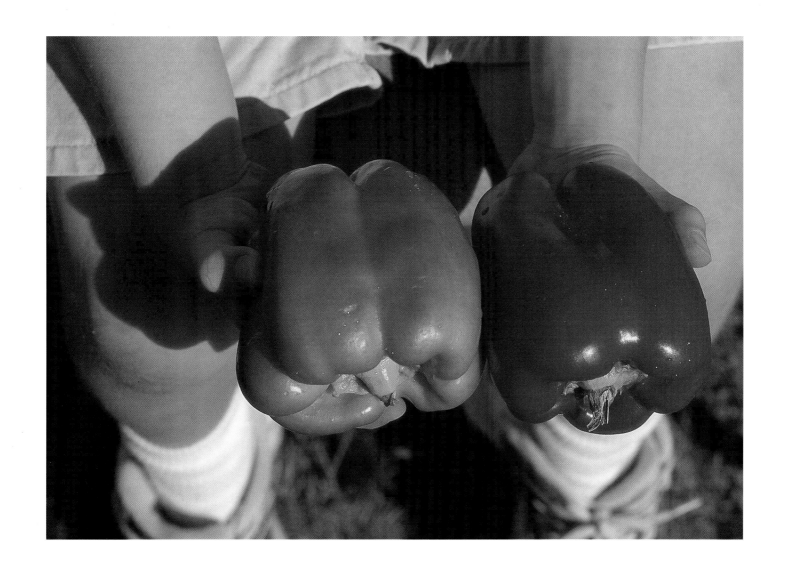

What colors are these peppers?

Green and red.

What color are these seeds?

Brown.

What two colors
are these five
animals?

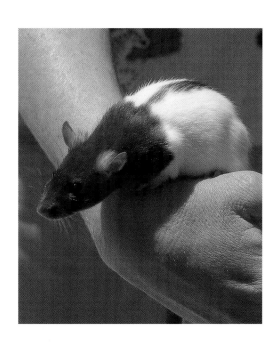

Black and white.

Aren't you happy we're surrounded by so much color?

To Frank Mozino at School-Time, and Denise Sontag at Community School District 27 and their great staffs. Thank you for making children's literature come alive for so many New York City schoolchildren.

Acknowledgments

Many thanks to all the great kids who lent their happy faces to the pages of this book: On the cover are kids from P.S. 225 in Rockaway Park, Queens, New York. Inside the book are Harry Forbes, Devon Swinburne, Libba Farrar, Deidre Hausslein, Austin Crandall, Johanna Poitevien, Elisabeth Balash, Miranda Balash, Esther Kim, and Mary Kim; kids from P.S. 225 in Rockaway Park, Queens, New York; and Pamela Becker's kindergarten class at the Brattleboro Central School, Brattleboro, Vermont. And thanks to the West River Aquarium and Pet Supply in Londonderry, Vermont, for the black-and-white snake and black-and-white rat.

Text and photographs © 2002 by Stephen R. Swinburne
All rights reserved

Published by Boyds Mills Press, Inc.
A Highlights Company
815 Church Street
Honesdale, Pennsylvania 18431
Printed in China
Visit our website at: www.boydsmillspress.com

Publisher Cataloging-in-Publication Data

Swinburne, Stephen R.
    What color is nature? / written and photographed by Stephen R. Swinburne. —1st ed.
[32] p. : col. photos. ;   cm.
Summary: A photographic essay featuring colors found in nature.
ISBN 1-56397-967-5 hardcover   1-59078-008-6 paperback
1. Nature photography — Juvenile literature. 2. Nature — Pictorial works. — Juvenile literature. (1. Nature photography. 2. Nature — Pictorial works.) I. Title.
508.0222 21   2002   CIP
2001092-590

First edition, 2002
The text of this book is set in 24-point Garamond.

10 9 8 7 6 5 4 3